The Affair:

How To Manage Sex In Singleness!

Breonna 'BG' Gildon

The Affair: How to Manage Sex in Singleness
Copyright © 2021 by Breonna Gildon

Printed in the United States of America

ISBN: (paperback) 978-0-578-95959-7
ISBN: (ebook) 978-0-578-95960-3

Published by Joseph's Ministry, LLC (www.josephsministryllc.com)

Photography by Harris Media Company

Scripture quotations marked NLT are taken from the Holy Bible, New Living Translation, copyright 1996, 2004, 2007, 2015 by Tyndale House Foundation. Used by permission of Tyndale House Publishers, Inc., Carol Stream, Illinois 60188. All rights reserved.

Scripture quotations taken from the Amplified® Bible (AMP), Copyright © 2015 by The Lockman Foundation. Used by permission. www.lockman.org

Scripture quotations from The Authorized (King James) Version. Rights in the Authorized Version in the United Kingdom are vested in the Crown. Reproduced by permission of the Crown's patentee, Cambridge University Press

This edition of the King James Authorized Version was paragraphed with sub-headings added by the British and Foreign Bible Society in 1954 and released again as a special edition in 2011.

BFBS additions © 2011 British and Foreign Bible Society

This text is maintained by the British and Foreign Bible Society

All rights reserved. No part of this publication may be reproduced, distributed, or transmitted in any form or by any means, including photocopying, recording, or other electronic or mechanical methods, without the prior written permission of the author, Breonna Gildon, except in the case of brief quotations embodied in critical reviews and certain other noncommercial uses permitted by copyright law. For permission requests, write to the author, addressed "Attention: Permissions Coordinator," at the address below.

Empower Her Ministries, LLC.
6910 S. Yorktown Ave.
#2925
Tulsa, OK 74170

I thank God for giving me the words to empower.

TABLE OF CONTENTS

Prologue: The Affair 7

I. Practical Steps To Maintain Purity

Chapter 1: Know Your Why 13

Chapter 2: Surrender 29

Chapter 3: Your Tribe, Your Vibe! 49

Chapter 4: Managing Sexual Triggers 65

II. How To Sustain Joy In Purity

Chapter 5: Stop Competing Against Time! 91

Chapter 6: Who U Were Is Not Who U Are! 103

Chapter 7: What Happens If You Fall? 111

III. Being Bold & Confident In Purpose

Chapter 8: Speak It! 121

- Bonus Section 123
- Acknowledgements 127
- Testimonials 131
- Sources 135
- About The Author 137

Prologue

You are not alone...in fact...I am just like you!

Staring up at the ceiling I could not wrap my mind around how did I arrive to the same starting point of defeat! It wasn't like I didn't try, I just couldn't come to grip with the source, other than me personally.

With a deep breath, I mustered to push myself up and out of the bed I was lying in and decided to head to church. It was Sunday morning, so I figured why not.

I had recently made a commitment to not have sex until marriage and I had just engaged sexually! Yet, no matter how bad I felt in the moment the new church I had been visiting always seemed to provide the right encouragement I needed to get me through the day.

As I walked to the bathroom, every step I took defined my walk of shame as lies began to form inside of my mind,

> "Your weakness to self-pleasure will always control you."
> "You don't deserve to be loved without struggling."
> "Nobody will love you, the real you."

I wanted better for myself!

It took no more than an hour and I was located right in the church's sanctuary entrance. A greeter walked up to me with the most welcoming smile while directing me to sit in a seat a couple rows not too far from the main platform.

The worship team was just wrapping up their performance and I was grateful. I needed time before the pastor would come on the stage to say a quick prayer from the type of morning I had.
The only words I could say was,
'God, I'm sorry. Forgive me.'

Not too soon later, the lead pastor transitioned on to the stage to start the introduction of his Sunday's message. Ironically, he introduced the topic of the day which was sex!

Every part of my being instantly started to fight for me to leave the church's building. However, I didn't want to be 'that obvious person'.

Comparatively something within me that I couldn't recognize was keeping me there. The feeling was familiar because I had felt it prior to me engaging sexually.

Without delay, more lies began to flood my mind,

'Your body count is too high for anyone to love you.'
'You're damaged.'
'You will never be enough.'

Then I heard, 'Surrender.'

My focus shifted back to the pastor on stage. He profoundly shared, 'Surrender your sexual desires to God. Ask Him to help you manage them.'

I was completely dumbfounded, yet I knew it wasn't a coincidence that I was hearing what I was hearing.
For the very first time in my life, I went to the creator of all, with a dire need that included sex.

A simple prayer escaped silently from my lips, "Lord, forgive me. Help me to manage my sexual desires."

Right then, I made the decision to trust God with all I had left. Releasing my hands off of life's steering wheel and upgraded into autopilot as Him leading the navigation!

Three years of no sex, no masturbation, and no pornography. That is where I am today.

Has the process been tough? Yes!
Am I really waiting for a specific time to have any form of sex again? Absolutely!
Do I still crave sex? Absolutely!!!

In fact, I think about it every day! Yet, I am choosing to wait in expectation and trust that this time, with God's help, I can manage sex in singleness because I never want to experience the shame of being physical.

The expectation I have I desire to give to you throughout the pages of this book!

As you continue on reading, I will give you purity tips within three sections:

*Practical Steps To Maintain Purity
*Practical Steps To Sustain Joy In Purity

And, finally...

*Be Bold and Confident In Purpose

Think of me as your new spiritual big sister who has literally done it all and is ready to equip you with all you need so you too can learn how to effectively manage sex in your singleness.

Now, get ready, Honey Bunches! You are soon about to start on a journey of becoming a greater you.

I. Practical Steps To Maintain Purity

Chapter 1

Knowing Your Purpose Helps You To Keep Going!

I may not know you, but I bet I can guess one thing about your purity journey without you even telling me. Now, I'm quite competitive!

For this reason, I am so confident my guess is right that you'll have to continue this entire book from cover to cover, with an open mind, of course. My guess is growing up you were more familiar with the word abstinence before hearing about celibacy.

No worries, me too! Now, a deal is a deal.

Keep on reading, my love!

Whether you're like me and grew up heavily involved in church or your family slept in on Sundays, abstinence is very common for our culture to first introduce to children as teenagers. I believe introducing ways to practice safe sex such as abstinence until marriage is a great early approach in helping people avoid heartbreaks, STIs, and unplanned pregnancies!

However, those of us who were secretly exposed to sex earlier than our 13th birthday were more than likely left with unwanted sexual desires to handle on our own. Not realizing we could have managed sex more effectively by starting over in purity with celibacy.

To put it differently, when we finally heard about abstinence, we may have already substituted sex with unhealthy practices like self-pleasure. Or, secretly watched pornography due to being unaware of how to handle sexual cravings life revealed to us prematurely.

As a result, we entered these dangerous gateways in hopes our sexual urges would vanish. In reality, what you and I both know is during those moments in self-pleasure only fulfilled us temporarily.

We were still left with cravings of getting what our parents, mentors, or church leaders strongly suggested for marriage, sex. This may of also led us going back to masturbation or pornography due to the guilt of already being physical and wanting to release what our body naturally craved, sex!

When we finally heard about abstinence, we may have experienced mixed emotions due to us thinking we were either not worthy of purity or felt compelled to do what everyone else was doing! The guilt more than likely left us feeling less confident to believe we could actually go through with purity.

Now, there's no judgement whatsoever! Like I stated within my first sentence, I am just like you. If you noticed, I said "we" a lot because I too, fell victim to lust.

I ventured on many trips of premarital sex and masturbation. You see, when I was introduced to the word abstinence, it was explained to me as a practice for a person to not have any sexual contact until marriage...
...which is true...
...However, when I finally became aware of the word abstinence, I felt "Well, I already failed!" and didn't believe it was possible for me to have a fresh start in purity.

I had already spent years repeating sexual habits and "slip ups" hoping time would eventually mature me to make better decisions! In spite of, I kept on the same lust-filled cycle, dated the same types of people, and held on to the same brokenness.

To me, choosing lust was like having an Affair. No matter how bad I wanted to stay committed in my relationship with Christ I didn't want to end The Affair because of the thrill of it all.

It wasn't until I discovered how to surrender my sexual desires to God through celibacy and later transitioned on to a journey in abstinence where I was able to break free from The Affair!

In return, God revealed to me a lot of wisdom that I'd love to share with you on living in purity: God's way.

Whether this is your first, second or final attempt at purity, I believe what I have to share with you is going to help you stay committed to a lifestyle of purity in your single season.

First things first, I want you to understand the full definitions of celibacy and abstinence and why I believe it's more beneficial to start your purity journey in celibacy and then move forward into abstinence.

According to Google, Celibacy is a process a person chooses to abstain from sexual interactions and marriage. Now, I'm sure you are wondering why am I sharing this first and why is celibacy more beneficial for you at the start of your purity journey!

Quite often, I believe many who start off in purity make this one little mistake by doing the following:

"Being celibate while praying for God to send a future spouse."

Now, I am an advocate to pray for your future spouse, however, let me tell you why this is a BIG No No in celibacy! If you are praying for God to send your future spouse while being celibate, I want to end a frustration you might have.

Let me repeat the definition of celibacy again:

Celibacy is a process a person chooses to abstain from sexual relations and marriage.

In other words, I believe when you choose to say 'I am celibate.' Your actions are saying 'I am choosing to take time to not involve myself in any form of sexual relations or marriage...including everything that comes with the process to be married...like dating!

By saying you are celibate, the words you say becomes your reality to be content in being single, alone, and living in the purpose God has for you.

As also stated in Proverbs 18:21, "there is the power of life in death in our tongues." Meaning, what you say will be!

I am not saying this to scare you, however, I want you to be mindful of how powerful your words really are.

Therefore, by choosing celibacy, you will be prepared for its entire process, not just being without the physical!

With this in mind, I want you to be also aware of how amazing the benefits are for starting your purity journey in celibacy will be for you.

Once again, when you choose celibacy, you are making a decision to not engage in any form of sexual relations while not involving yourself with marriage. As you may know, engaging in sexual interactions or dating can sometimes influence your decisions. (Proverbs 31:3)

Think about your first heart break. And, I'm not referring to the moment you discovered 'Chick-fil-A' wasn't open on Sundays!

Before your first heartbreak relationship ended, you can admit you gave a lot of yourself to the person you loved. You may have grew into a routine of doing most things that that person liked.

You may have even held back parts of who you really are, gave pieces of yourself away, or broke certain values you held. The reason was simple: you wanted to make sure you did your best to keep that person happy!

Eventually, you learned happiness doesn't last forever. The heartbreak may have also left you regretting the relationship in the first place or worse afraid to ever try to love again.

If this is you, I want you to know God loves you so much that when He gave His one and only son Jesus as a sacrifice on the cross, He did it with you in mind! He had already factored in everything you could ever do and still loves you. (John 3:16)

If you haven't already figured out, I believe celibacy is more beneficial for you in the start of your singleness because it's a process to learn you before saying I do.

And, I'm not referring to marriage!

Celibacy helps you to give yourself permission to say 'I do like this' 'I do enjoy that.' 'I do see myself doing this for the rest of my life!' 'Wow! I didn't know that I do help people in this way.'

In other words, practicing celibacy grants you time to discover things you enjoy, such as your God-given talents, and develop those gifts to enhance God's kingdom. This is done even before deciding to be aligned to anyone else's purpose or taking on unnecessary shame from things or people who were never intended in God's purpose for you in the first place!

Even the Apostle Paul, a bomb.com Apostle in the Bible, explained the benefits of celibacy when he said, "...a woman who is no longer married or has never been married can be devoted to the Lord and holy in body and in spirit." 1 Corinthians 7:34

No matter who you are, I believe Apostle Paul's logic can still be considered valuable if you choose celibacy today!

Here's another example, think of a Pope or a Priest. Have you ever heard of a married Pope or a married Priest? No, Popes and Priests are well-known to be single men of God who are devoted to enhancing the kingdom of God by using their gifts while remaining faithful to their celibacy vow.

Like Popes and Priests, think of your celibacy journey as a great start of using your gifts pressure free of romantic temptations or commitment! Beginning purity in celibacy creates a focus of learning and building a better version of yourself for your life's purpose: God's will for you.

Therefore, if you do have the desire of marriage, your celibacy journey will have you more confident in who you are in God ever before inviting someone along to join your life's journey.

Celibacy also gives you time to grow stronger emotionally, financially, mentally, physically, and spiritually!

You are even free to heal from trauma you may have experienced as a child in which I'll explain more in a later chapter! Now, let me share with you on abstinence and its benefits to your purity.

According to Google, Abstinence is when a person chooses not to have sex. Period! I believe abstinence should be the next step after celibacy in your purity process only if you desire marriage. Once you've spent enough time in purity where you are confident in who you are, strong enough in your personal boundaries (no matter who is watching), and living in purpose on purpose, I believe you are only then free to transition to abstinence!

Similar to celibacy, abstinence is a time for pursuing purpose and remaining sex-free. On the other hand, in abstinence this is a time that gives you the freedom to also began gathering data from prospective candidates for marriage to see if they are aligned to God's will for you. Thank Dr. Dharius Daniels' YouTube channel for teaching me this!

Now, I'm sure you may have wondered, "How do I know so much on celibacy and abstinence?". As I shared in the prologue, recently I transitioned to abstinence.

I spent well over two years in committed celibacy after learning from over two decades of pure failure to The Affair! It is only by God's grace I have been able to manage no sex and no masturbation. Meaning, with God's help, I have a lot of tips for you to become successful in purity!

So, let's begin.

I want you to take a moment to think about why you would like to/ why are you choosing a lifestyle of purity.

Did you experience a recent break up?
Were you inspired by watching your favorite YouTube vlogger?
Have you heard a sermon lately on purity?
Did a famous couple's love story make you want to hold out?
Are you tired of being entangled to The Affair?
What has made you decide to take a vow in purity?

Honestly, there is no right or wrong answer!

Even if your answer is a failed relationship or inspiration from someone, you need to be aware of the reason for your commitment to be pure. Your very answer in why you are choosing purity is what I call "Your Why".

For example, in a good marriage, when a bride and groom make the decision to be married, they have entered an agreement between themselves, one another, and God to be committed until death. Once the couple has joined together their bond is intact for life!

The legitimate reasons the bond may be broken prematurely is in the case of infidelity or death.

Meaning, the married couple must stay within their covenant even if their emotions don't feel up to par as a fairytale's Happily Ever After! The couple's marriage covenant is the "Why" in keeping them together.

No matter how bad the husband snores at night, a good wife will choose to stay in her marriage and honor the vows she made to her husband. No matter how much the wife complains about her job, a good husband will choose to stay in his marriage and honor the vows he made to his wife.

No matter if the husband or wife sees someone physically more attractive than their spouse, a good couple will stay committed to one another and honor the vows they made to their spouse: because of Their Why!

Similar to the good husband and wife, while choosing purity, there will be times where you want to give up or give in to going against Your Why. Once you have discovered Your Why, you will experience many temptations coming your way. It will be a challenge, but Your Why will give you the reassurance to keep steady on your commitment to purity!

Your Why will quickly snap you out of making a hasty decision based on emotions that you could possibly regret right after engaging in The Affair or for the rest of your life!

Now, I'm not sure how familiar you are with Proverbs 29:18, but it is stated, "Where there's no vision, people perish!" Your Why is what keeps your purity journey in a consistent focus, such as having vision, and has the capability to produce freedom not only for you, but through you!

Without knowing the purpose behind why you are choosing purity makes it easy for you to quit or kill your purity commitment. The very thing that ignited your heart to choose purity may have been the starting point to your journey, however, knowing Your Why will give you the strength to sustain it!

Your future self deserves for you to succeed in purity!

You deserve to be free from sexual impurity simply because you are a child of God. Like in John 8:36 says, 'So if the Son sets you free, you are truly free.' There is no reason for The Affair, or lust, to hold you captive any longer.

Your debt has already been paid...in full!

If I can be honest with you, during these last three years in purity has been surprisingly easier than any of my previous attempts. The reason is God helped me to understand the importance of discovering My Why. Shortly after, I made the decision to no longer want a dependence on The Affair but to start anew with Christ leading me every step of the way!

You see, my previous attempts in purity were birthed by being hurt from failed relationships. At the time, I was only 'holding out' (sexually) due to pain and trauma I suffered.

I also tried purity in other attempts hoping to gain the approval of others. I'd hope if I could be like other people just maybe by following their paths I, too, would end my commitment to The Affair!

However, with every attempt, I constantly caved into The Affair due to unmet expectations and unrealistic pressures I placed on myself. When I finally chose purity for my freedom from The Affair and kept in mind of My Why, I felt and still feel confident in not giving into former sexual habits or needs.

It is only by God's grace that I have found that freedom from The Affair. And, I believe the same will happen for you too!

God's freedom was extending to you when Jesus was raised from the dead. You no longer have to suffer to The Affair when Jesus has already given you the power to overcome!

Before rushing off to the next chapter, I would love for you to take time to evaluate all what we've discussed so far. In fact, for every chapter of this book you will find a small section at the end called Nuggets to help you refresh and reflect on the chapter's key points for you to apply in your purity journey.

For your first reflection, I have some Purpose Nuggets, to share with you to help keep your purity vision alive! With God, you will be able to overcome The Affair.

You can do it this time, I believe in you.

Purpose Nuggets

Knowing Your Purpose Helps To Keep Your Purity Vision Alive. What Is It About Purity That Attracts You?

_____

_____

_____

_____

_____

_____

_____

Purpose Nuggets

Abstinence And Celibacy Are Similar Yet Different. Which Purity Process Do You Believe Is Best For You Right Now?

_____

_____

_____

_____

_____

_____

_____

Purpose Nuggets

Write Below 3 Personal Affirmations On Purity

(Ex. 'I am a master at self-control.')

_____

_____

_____

_____

_____

_____

_____

Purpose Nuggets

Find 3 Bible Scriptures That Inspire You About Self Control & Write Them In The Below Section.

_____

_____

_____

_____

_____

_____

_____

Chapter 2

The first response to any form of healing begins with surrender.

Could you imagine being made by God to do something against your will? I believe many of us who are or has taken the purity route have thought about this once or twice!

There are times when a sexual urge can get so strong the thought of God being able to instantly shut down your sexual thoughts or body functions sound appeasing. Hoping God could somehow press a pause button from Heaven to handle your sexual emotions until marriage or the grave!

After discovering My Why, I was enlightened by a former Pastor of a spiritual truth: he profoundly shared that the desire to have sex wasn't bad, I just needed God's help in managing.

That's right! Mentally, it was like an instant lightbulb went off that never lit up in my mind before. The emotions behind being able to experience sex were so strong that the very idea God being the Creator of all never once included sex to me.

Prior to purity, Trey Songz and Pretty Ricky's Blue Star album were my go to for understanding sex! Or, on a good day I would listen to some H-Town's Knockin' Boots or watch movies such as Love Jones.

Yeah, I had a wild imagination!

Basically, prior to my former Pastor's revelation, the only time I considered using God and sex in the same sentence were limited to my prayer of Him helping me to not 'do it' again!

I'm ashamed to say God was my last resort in seeking sexual wisdom. Can you relate?

Have you ever had a time in your life where the only time you added God into the equation of sex was asking Him to forgive you for falling victim to The Affair?

Somewhere along participating with The Affair made you ashamed and you felt compelled to seek God after being involved instead of before. I believe many of us have.

In fact, this isn't anything new! In Genesis 3, you can find the very first story of a person falling victim to temptation: Eve.

Within the next few passages of scriptures, let's take a look at how Eve was enticed by temptation and learn from her mistakes to help you overcome The Affair:

Genesis 3:1 The serpent was the shrewdest of all the wild animals the Lord God had made. One day he asked the woman, "Did God really say you must not eat the fruit from the garden?'

Genesis 3:2 "Of course we may eat fruit from the trees in the garden," the woman replied.

Genesis 3:3 It's only the fruit from the tree in the middle of the garden that we are not allowed to eat. God said, 'You must not eat it or even touch it; if you do, you will die.'

Genesis 3:4 'You won't die!' the serpent replied to the woman.

Genesis 3:5 'God knows that your eyes will be opened as soon as you eat it, and you will be like God, knowing both good and evil.'

Genesis 3:6 The woman was convinced. She saw that the tree was beautiful and its fruit looked delicious, and she wanted the wisdom it would give her. So she took some of the fruit and ate it.

Now, let's take a pause right here!

Did you catch where our sister, Eve, made her error?

If you look closely, the answer is found in Genesis 3:6.

The woman was convinced. She saw that the tree was beautiful and its fruit looked delicious, and she wanted the wisdom it would give her. 'SO SHE TOOK SOME OF THE FRUIT AND ATE IT.'

I believe the main reason why Eve fell into temptation because she didn't follow a key principle in managing temptation: Seeking God, first!

Seeking God first diminishes your chances of being the victim to temptation.

I believe Eve did not commit the first sin by looking at the fruit. She didn't even commit the first sin by wanting the wisdom it would give her. The main reason behind Eve falling into temptation was due to her decision to seek herself first and not God.

Matthew 6:33 But seek ye first the kingdom of God and his righteousness; and all these things shall be added unto you.

Eve acted in sin because she trusted and made a decision based on her own judgment over God's counsel. When it comes to your purity journey, seeking God first is essential, regularly!

Opportunities will come every day. Temptation to engage in sexual sin will present itself to you.

Like Eve, some opportunities and temptations may appear to you as delicious as the fruit in the garden! Seeking God first is beneficial for you because you will be aware of choosing what is from God and avoiding what is not from Him.

When you seek God first, He will help you to succeed in all you do, and that is not just limited to purity!

What Does Seeking God look like?

You can seek God in many ways! God is omnipresent. Meaning, he is everywhere at the same time. Therefore, He is always near and available to you. (Psalms 46:1)

When you seek God first, you are outwardly expressing your heart's desire to surrender to His plan knowing He will be everything you need and more. Seeking God can be done through prayer, fasting, worship, reading the Bible, the Holy Spirit, and more!

However, for the next few and final pages of this chapter I would like to focus with you on the following: prayer, fasting, worship, reading the Bible, and the Holy Spirit.

Prayer is your direct line to heaven!

Have you ever had a problem and you tried calling a close friend or relative to help you only to be greeted by their voice mail? The nerve, right? However, I have great news for you, there are no voicemails to heaven!

When you pray to God, there is an instant pick up on His direct line. Meaning, he will answer when you call Him every time.

Prayer can be one of your greatest tools, especially in defeating The Affair! Every day you will need God's assistance to help manage your purity journey because let's face it living the purity lifestyle is a challenge.

When it comes to seeking God, prayer is how we, his children, communicate to Him. Once you are a child of God, you can simply say, 'God, I need you.' or 'God, help me.'

God is so faithful because you don't need a long drawn out prayer for Him to listen! When you seek Him in prayer, He will provide you with the very thing(s) that you need.

In response, you must simply have faith in Him.
(Mark 11:24)

The Bible also lets you know to never stop praying (1 Thessalonians 5:17). By sharing your gratitude, asking for help, and being intentional in prayer daily, you will be surprised by how easy purity will become for you.

Make sure to be consistent in seeking God in prayer. Just like your close friend or family member, God loves to hear from you and He loves for you to hear from Him too!

Fasting is your faith in discipline form.

There's a saying I grew up hearing within the church community,

'Some things only come by praying and fasting!'

This 'saying' originates from the story in the Bible (Mark 9) where Jesus heals a demon possessed man after His disciples were not able to. The disciples were a bit confused on why they couldn't heal the once demon possessed man and the above saying was Jesus' response to them. *How gangsta!*

Fasting is a way you can seek God through temporarily eliminating things that you enjoy, such as certain foods and etc., to be more intentional in prayer, reading the Bible, and worship. Therefore, you can seek God through fasting by blocking out all distractions to hear Him more clearly.

I know. I know. This doesn't sound like a fun way to seek God. However, the benefits are indeed rewarding!

The bible even shares the regularity of fasting.
'And when you fast, don't make it obvious, as the hypocrites do, for they try to look miserable and disheveled so people will admire them for their fasting. I tell you the truth, that is the only reward they will ever get.'
-Matthew 6:16

The duration of the fast is up to you! You may choose one day to fast, a three day fast, a week fast, twenty-one days of fasting, or more! What is key is found in the words 'When you fast'.

'When you fast' gives a statement, *By Jesus,* that fasting can happen as often as reading the Bible, gathering for worship, or spending time in prayer! You see there may be a time in your purity journey where you feel God is silent.

Seeking God through fasting gives you time in total isolation from distractions to hear God clearly. Because let's face it, God is never really silent! He is omnipresent, He is everywhere at the same time. (Psalm 139:7-10)

However, I believe many of us who chooses the purity journey will become so involved in various activities, such as serving in ministry, working, starting a business or etc. The activities we choose may help to keep our minds focused off of.. *you know, staying away from The Affair :)*

Though we may do these things with good intentions, if we are honest, these routines can sometimes drain out the voice of God. With this being said, the busyness of life can make it seem like God is far or even silent!

Therefore, fasting can be an essential tool you can use in your purity journey to draw you closer to the nearness of God. Fasting will also help remove all things that are filling up space in your life and make room to allow God's presence to overflow.

In your purity journey, you will need God's constant direction in all that you do! By you intentionally seeking God through fasting, you will always have access to hear clearly from God on everything you need.

Worship is not simply your favorite song...it's your lifestyle!

When you are faced with something difficult or beyond your control, what is the first thing that you do? Do you reach out to a friend? A family member? Social media? What is your initial response?

You would be surprised by how many times my answer has been all of the above! I have repeatedly made the decision to seek others before God while knowing He could reveal what I truly needed. Now, if you have done this before, welcome to the tribe! No one is perfect, including those of us who choose to follow Christ and God's way to overcome The Affair. However, let me help you break this cycle how God helped me.

No matter what opportunity. No matter how big or how small choose to seek God first! Not family. Not friends. Not even social media. His approval will lead you to everything you need and more!

Do you recall the story of our sister Eve and the Matthew 6:33 verse? God wants the best for you (3 John 1:2). Trust His plan and you can experience this through the art of worship!

And so, dear brothers and sisters, I plead with you to give your bodies to God because of all he has done for you. Let them be a living and holy sacrifice—the kind he will find acceptable. This is truly the way to *worship* him. Romans 12:1

Worship is your lifestyle. Worship is adoration to God. Worship is expressed in the way you live and the decisions you make.

When you choose to worship God, you are letting Him know you crave and trust His will, His way!

Reading the Bible is your direct source to living.

The next way you can also seek God is through reading His word. Now, you probably already knew this right? I could even argue that reading the Bible is one of the best ways you can seek God because God is His word.

John 1:1 let us know that 'In the beginning the Word already existed. The Word was with God, and the Word was God.'

Therefore, you can find Him by simply opening up His book!

I understand you may have your favorite Minister of the Gospel. However, you will experience moments in your purity journey where you need a word from God Himself.

The Bible grants you that access!

The Holy Spirit is your guide.

There was once a time I sat listening to a sermon online where the pastor shared a series of passages in the Bible about hearing from God. In His message, he stated how certain people, at the time, would carry special stones to discern a yes or no.

Any time the people needed an answer the stones would either light up or remain dimmed in response to their requests. If the stones lit up, it meant the Holy Spirit was telling the people yes.

If the stones didn't light up, the reply was no. Many times those individuals used the intricate stones concerning war, traveling, and etc. I thought to myself, *"How amazing!"*

Shortly after the message, I hurried home excited to discuss what I heard with my father. Ever since I was a young girl, my dad and I have this thing where our most thought-provoking conversations happen in his car.

Our tradition first began on car rides to school and continue to this very day! For some reason, I recall my dad and I being in his car not too soon after I arrived home. More than likely, I may had traveled with him to pick up Sunday dinner for our family.

Either way, I was ready to converse about the sermon message I'd heard. Usually, whenever we are in his car, he has something interesting to share for me to receive spiritually.

On this particular occasion, I was *pumped!* After the hundreds of times I had listened to his wisdom I was ready to beat him to the punch! Our car ride was coming to an end as my dad pulled up into my parent's driveway.

Once the car was in park, I sat up proudly in the plush leather car seat. As my dad took his keys out the ignition, I began to open up my mouth and confidently proceeded to explain to him the Sunday message I'd heard.

I even went on in further details about how I believed it would be amazing if it were possible to have a few of those stones to use in this generation. Laughter. That was my dad's exact reaction!

Puzzled and instantly filled with embarrassment I couldn't understand what was so amusing to my father after I had just dropped this *fiyah* word I not too long ago received! Therefore, I waited to hear what my dad had to following up with. Unbeknownst to me, I wasn't ready for what he would soon share.

"Breonna, we have better access. We, *believers of Christ*, have the Holy Spirit who He lives inside of us. Even if we had the opportunity to have those stones now, people would still do what they want."

I pondered for a brief moment and considered what my dad said. He was telling the truth!

You may be wondering "How so? How can I determine when the Holy Spirit is speaking to me?"

Answer this. Have you ever felt a strong feeling not to do or do something.

For example, let's say you wake up from your sleep to prepare for a productive day. Maybe you are heading to work or a meeting. Maybe you are heading to school. Either way you have a big day ahead of you.

As you are choosing your outfit, 'something tells you or a feeling comes over you to grab an umbrella.' However, you ignore the nudge because you checked the weather the previous night. *Which said the weather would be sunny all day long... 98 Degrees to be exact!*

Also, you don't feel like carrying around an umbrella with you all day. Therefore, you proceed to select your outfit, head off to your productive day without including the umbrella. Later in the day, the unthinkable happens.

Once you arrive to your destination, you step outside of your vehicle and rain begins to violently pour down from the sky. Then, you think to yourself, 'Something told me to grab that umbrella!' Well, let me tell you that 'something' is the Holy Spirit.

In your purity process, 'the something told me experience' happens quite often. It usually comes right when you are thinking about responding to that "come over" or "u up?" text.

There will be a voice or feeling in the back of your mind that will tell you to not respond or LEAVE THAT PERSON ALONE.

It's like no matter how many times you try to ignore and move forward with The Affair that tiny voice always come back screaming "Don't give in!" Meaning, the feeling or voice is directing you to be committed to purity or instructing you to remove yourself in times of temptation.

That is the Holy Spirit! Now, I understand the name sounds a bit spooky, but the Holy Spirit is not a ghost. In fact, He is meant to help you, live in you, and lead you in all truth. (John 14:16-17)

If I can be even more transparent with you, in my previous attempts at purity, I knew when The Holy Spirit was speaking to me. I may have not recognized Him as the Holy Spirit.

However, determining right from wrong existed inside of me even when I had my first glance at a pornographic movie. Seriously, looking at two naked people on tv kissing each other was not something my parents would encourage me to watch! In fact, as a young girl, I remember them forcing me to look away from "love scenes" in certain movie films or tv shows.

When I finally had the opportunity to see what was the big deal, there was a 'sense' I felt that conveyed, "You shouldn't watch this." The older I got the more my desire of The Affair grew the more I would ignore "that sense" on the inside of me.

Don't ignore The Holy Spirit on the inside of you!

The Holy Spirit is an aide to help you to seek God and live your very best in a life of abundance.

To help you understand this even better, whenever the next time you are faced with the temptation of The Affair ask and answer yourself the following question:

"Does this voice or feeling align with The Word of God?"

This actually brings us to the final nugget of this chapter: dependence or better known as surrender.

Being strong in purity comes by you fully depending on God.

God knows what you need. God made you in His image; therefore, He knows how strong your desires are!

Choosing to seek God regularly in purity will help you avoid the trauma of participating with The Affair.

Take these next few moments to think how your life could look like if you allowed God to lead in you in purity. Now, of course, I am not going to ask you this question without giving you a guide!

Surrendering can certainly appear like a challenging task. This is why I created a few extra Nuggets for you to take a moment to answer this chapter's topic on Surrender.

❧Surrender Nuggets❧

What has stopped you in the past to surrender your sexual urges to God?

_____

_____

_____

_____

_____

_____

_____

🕊Surrender Nuggets🕊

How would you like for God to help you in purity right now?

_____

_____

_____

_____

_____

_____

_____

Surrender Nuggets

The health of your purity relies on your intentionality to God's word. What is one way you plan to seek God today, this week, or this month?

🐦Surrender Nuggets🐦

What has stopped you in the past to surrender your sexual urges to God?

_____
_____
_____
_____
_____
_____
_____

🕊Surrender Nuggets🕊

You read that God is omnipresent a few times throughout this chapter. After reading this chapter, what is one thing that God is speaking to you?

_____

_____

_____

_____

_____

_____

_____

Chapter 3

The people who surround you can either make or break your destiny.

What about your friends? 1991 was a great year! Besides God creating me in His image to enter the world, one of the greatest trendsetting music groups, TLC, recorded a popular song that started off like the following:

"Every now and then, I get a little crazy, that's not the way it's supposed to be. Sometimes my vision is a little hazy, I can't tell who I should trust or just who I let trust me."

I love this song specifically not only because of its catchy beat and lyrics. The song's title is a question I ask myself often throughout my purity journey: What about your friends? You see, when it comes to ending The Affair, it's so important who is surrounding you.

Oh, you thought surrendering to God was just it, No, no, no!

Believe it or not, our friends can be some of the most influential people in our world, especially when it comes to decisions based on self-control!

Don't believe me?

Mmhm! Let you decide to start a diet. Your inspiration may have came from a health related commercial and you were instantly convinced to try out the new product being advertised.

Perhaps, you were scrolling on social media and caught a warm post of Tabitha Brown inspiring you to try out one of her tasty vegan recipes. Isn't she simply amazing? Okay, off topic back to the diet!

Just maybe you were in the grocery store shopping and saw one of your old classmates from high school who happens to still look the way they did 5, 10, 20, 30, 40 years ago! While you two were chatting about life and what not, you couldn't help yourself to ask the question, "What's your secret?"

Without hesitation, your classmate senses your true intent of acquiring health-related knowledge and shares with you their ability to master self-control. They even go further in details on how they not only workout, but they've decided to remove dairy from their diet and other fatty foods to stay physically fit.

Now, I can go on and on with scenarios, but you get the idea!

Once the thought of a diet gets inside of your mind, you mentally decide to stay committed with the belief this new lifestyle will help you. Months may even go by and you have been surprisingly intentional with the diet!

In the beginning, keeping up with certain healthy eating patterns was a challenge. Yet, the more you stay committed to the diet the greater you feel.

Bold and confident to simply be, is all you are!

You may even notice a few physical improvements in your body. You're not as sluggish; you're filled with so much energy! Mentally, you notice how positive your outlook on the world is becoming. You are completely a new person!

Well, one day, your best friend, who lives out of town, decides to surprise and visit you for your birthday weekend. In the midst of joy in catching up, your best friend says they want to pay for dinner at a local restaurant.

Instantly, you are reminded this specific restaurant is well-known for its delicious food, but its menu doesn't have any of the healthy options you've grown accustomed to. You share with your best friend about your new diet and how you've been staying away from such places.

Then, your friend says to live a little, lighten up, and have some fun! You deserve this one moment to enjoy. Are you going to stick to the diet?

The sad truth is many of us won't! No matter how much we know the new diet is something good to keep practicing, the pressure to no longer continue will most likely cause a sense of urgency leading us to eventually cave.

The more our friend asks and pleads with us to indulge in a night of freedom from our diet the easier our friend's influence will weaken our control.

Many of us will even begin to convince ourselves why it's so important to enjoy the moment! The more pressure we receive the more our thoughts will start sounding like, "Well, it is for my best friend". "They did take the time to show how they care by visiting me". "It is my birthday". "I do deserve to have a little fun". "It is only for the weekend."

Finally, the diet is no longer a priority; a weekend of fun away from our diet sounds better than our very own personal commitment. Besides, we can always choose to recommit to a healthy journey after this one time of caving, right?

Do you see where I am going? Does this sound familiar to your purity journey? Have you ever gave in to a moment of temptation based on the influence of a relationship?

I'm sure everyone has at one point! However, no matter the past, you are in the right position right now to take control and decide who is going to help you manage The Affair. Take a moment to evaluate your circle of friends.

What role do your friends play in your commitment to purity?

- How aware are they about you choosing purity?
- How often do you share your sexual triggers to them?
- How often do they offer to pray for you in low times?
- What are your friend's responses to the unexpected?
- What do your friend's other friendships look like?
- What are your friend's views on self-control?

In the light of answering those questions, I hope your responses are able to reveal who is beneficial to you during your purity process. It is so important to always be mindful of who is around you while you're choosing a lifestyle in purity!

In Proverbs 27:17, the Bible states, "As iron sharpens iron, so a friend sharpens a friend."

Taking a vow of celibacy or practicing abstinence is a stretching and challenging process. As beautiful as our culture and most social media influencers paint abstinence and celibacy, by no means is purity a cake walk!

You will experience moments where you don't want to be spiritually strong. You will experience moments where what you're used to (getting physical) sounds a lot better than praying and fasting!

After surrendering your sexual desires to God, Satan is going to try everything he has to cause you to give up! This Proverbs scripture is so vital especially in purity because you not only need the strength of God to remain pure, you need a solid tribe of people who believe in you, even when you don't believe in yourself!

Whenever a low mental moment arrives to convince you to cave in and you are craving physical pleasure...it's nice to say you can call on Jesus.

But, let's be real! There are times after seeking God you will still crave to give in to what your body is experiencing.
Having the aide of a faith-filled spiritual friend can give you the confidence you need to endure any sexual temptation! The Bible is also pretty clear on the benefits of having friends.

> "Two people are better off than one, for they can help each other succeed."(Ecclesiastes 4:9 NLT)

Your squad is a reflection of you! When you look at your friends do you see success, in purity?

In reality, there's not a day that goes by where the desire to have sex or masturbate doesn't cross my mind. I remember in the first six months of my current purity journey were filled with some of the most spiritually stretching moments I have ever had to endure.

My emotions were everywhere and I was a total hot mess. Literally!

I'm sure you can relate to this as well. I believe this happens to too many of us often in the beginning stages of purity because we are in a brand new process of allowing God to renew our minds from The Affair and depend on Him.

It's like trying to teach a grown adult a new skill or hobby! I'll share more with you on this topic in Chapter 6.

From time to time, I spent the early months in purity alone and confused on why on earth was it a challenge to handle my raging hormones. I would make sure to pray about what I was experiencing and made a routine to read the Bible on the regular! I called myself being intentional in my first purity attempts because I would "ask, pray, and seek God" hoping he would open the door to a more purified version of me! Yet, I would still hold on to my attachment with The Affair.

I expected my prayers eventually would lead and waltz me into a victory while having somewhat control. As a result, I was spiritually blocking the pathway to an answered prayer and didn't even realize it.

In other words, although I chose to surrender my sexual desires to God that didn't stop past images of viewing pornographic films or past sexual encounters to reoccur to me randomly.

By starting purity alone, there was no one there to "sharpen me". I was left exposed to every opportunity of the enemy without a friend!

In fact, I believe this was a very dangerous game to play. At any moment, I could have been weak and caved in due to pressure.

In due time, God revealed to me the error of my ways: I never shared what I was experiencing with anyone else! I had to submit to exercising the second Nugget in purity: intentional accountability.

In order to stay committed to purity, you need intentional accountability.

I define Intentional Accountability as the on purpose obligation to support a person's commitments. Meaning, intentional accountability is someone choosing to stay by a friend's side spiritually to help them reaching their friend's goals.

Once again, in purity you cannot do it alone! You need God and intentional accountability to help you to succeed. In fact, say this out loud wherever you are, "With God and intentional accountability, I will master purity."

Repeat this declaration and yes out loud, but this time don't worry about who is or who isn't around you and believe you will succeed in purity. Now, I want you to really think for a moment. How can you successfully stay committed to something if you are the only person who knows about your goal(s)?

Even the most well-known athletes are provided trainers and coaches to help perfect their crafts! Similar to professional athletes, having someone to be your sounding board will make you stronger and give you great power to combat every attack of the enemy in purity for you to win!

As a matter of fact, you may want to write the following scripture down and post on your mirror and it's found in James 5:16. It states,

> "Confess your sins to each other and pray for each other so that you may be healed. The earnest prayer of a righteous person has great power and produces wonderful results."

According to vocabulary.com, the word earnest is stated as "If you are earnest, it means you are serious about something." Making the decision for you to practice abstinence or take a vow of celibacy is a serious decision and moment for you, right?

Even if you're considering purity, I know the decision for you to try it out is mind blogging because saying no to something you desire sounds ludicrous!

Whether you are like me with celibacy being your last resort in conquering The Affair, abstinence is your first response, or you're on the fence about purity, this commitment is valuable to you. When you think of having something that is of great value, what's the first thing that comes to mind?

For me, I instantly think of gold! Now, don't judge me too hard. I am simply a girl from Oklahoma.

To give you a better understanding, I'll tell you why gold is valuable, how similar it is to your purity, how intentional accountability is identical to owning gold, and I believe you will be ready to reevaluate or completely eliminate your tribe to gain intentional accountability!

Now, are you ready?

First, gold is one of the most precious metals known to the world. When it comes to currency, most if not all, people have access to money such as coins or dollars. Once you get a Peso, Euro, Silver Dollar or Franklin in your hands it is yours to keep or trade for something of its value!

Gold is different. Not everyone has or owns real gold. I believe gold is so precious due to the process it has to endure in order to become valuable.

In fact, according to the European Precious Metals Federation, the average gold mine could take up to 10 or more years to even be ready to produce gold...not sell, produce! The very people who own real gold are few and are considered prestigious by many. You know, like famous people, kings, queens, and entertainers.

Now, in terms of money, unlike gold, almost anyone can have access to obtaining it for their own personal use by simply working to have it or randomly finding it on the side of the road. There is a process to money like mining, refining, melting, casting, and etc.

However, for a person to receive money in their hands is easier than receiving gold. Seriously, would you be more comfortable to ask someone for gold or a dollar?

In terms of your purity journey, I personally believe the way you are choosing to take care of your body emotionally, mentally, physically, and spiritually is of great value! You are literally denying your flesh for a certain period of your life in obedience to God to produce something great, like gold.

Since you are choosing purity, every day you gain more value to who you are than the day before. Because of your faithfulness and integrity to God's word, He will return His faithfulness and integrity back to you. (Psalms 18:25) And, that's Bible.

Yes, my friend your choice to choose purity was and is a valuable decision! Spiritually, I believe heaven's host of angels daily applaud you.

Your purity is gold. Now, you may be thinking why am I saying all of this to you. Here's the Nugget I want you to comprehend:

Your purity is rewarding.

Matthew 5:8 explains, "Blessed are those whose hearts are pure, for they will see God."

Once you are on your purity journey long enough you will begin to notice how practicing self-control through purity will greatly enhance other areas in your life. For example, you may notice how financially refined you are becoming by not eating out as much.

This is one of many ways how abstinence and celibacy are so vital in your singleness because you are developing in purity, not just physically! You may even notice how your journey inspires close friends along their spiritual walks as well. And, I believe God honors this on heaven and earth!

Intentional Accountability can help heal and reveal what you may not see.

Similar to gold, your purity is precious and desirable to obtain. However, there is a spiritual thief who has a daily intent to steal what God has deemed good in your life: your purity. The bible shares in the first half of John 10:10, "the enemy's purpose is to steal, kill, and destroy." Why am I sharing this with you?

I said it before and I will say it again. Your tribe, the people who surround you, should be as serious as you are about protecting your purity process. (Proverbs 20:7)

When you are feeling weak to temptation, you will need people spiritually fighting and blocking all temptations of the enemy alongside with you! If you have not already, take a moment to really reflect on those who surround you and determine who is your intentional accountability.

Intentional accountability also comes with a trusted people who are willing to go the extra mile. Meaning, those individuals who are your intentional accountability will even strengthen you through in prayer and fasting! When you have intentional accountability, your purity journey is literally your friend's purity journey.

It doesn't matter if your friend is married or single, this period in your life matters to them because they're believing God for your healing, peace, strength and most of all your purity! What about your friends?

Now, the following question I am about to ask you, you've answered on a previous page. However, I want to ask you once again, but I want you to dig a bit deeper.

When you think about your inner circle or community of friends, can you say they would be willing to pray for your abstinence or celibacy journey even without you telling them? Some of my most low moments in purity quickly turned to victory simply by the powerful prayers from my group of friends.

There were times I couldn't even think of nothing to say, yet God would lead a friend to call me. Within minutes, that same friend would be praying the very things that were detailed within my heart. The thing is none of my close friends are perfect by no means!

Each one has something they are progressing through life and I make sure to intercede for them as well. What I can say no matter what they all make sure to be intentional to my purity process. I know I am safe with them to share transparently and I feel confident to overcome The Affair with their help.

I challenge you to pay attention to how you feel the next time you speak about abstinence or celibacy with your friends. Make a mental note of the energy on the phone, in the car, or room. Did the atmosphere feel peaceful or were you experiencing butterflies that danced in your stomach?

Remember, your journey in purity is valuable. Make sure you are surrounded by spiritual warriors who will protect your purity by fighting temptations alongside with you.

Friendship Nuggets

What role does your friend(s) play in your purity journey?

_____

_____

_____

_____

_____

_____

_____

_____

Friendship Nuggets

What is your friend(s) prayer lifestyle look like?

_____
_____
_____
_____
_____
_____
_____
_____

Friendship Nuggets

How are the people who surround you valuable to you?

_____

_____

_____

_____

_____

_____

_____

Chapter 4

Your silence increases power to your sexual desires!

Let's talk about sex baby! Let's talk about you and me! By now, I'm sure you can tell I love all types of music. When it comes to maintaining purity, it's quite similar.

There are so many topics to discuss, yet my favorite is sex! You may be wondering, "Why is that?" "Shouldn't purity be a time for us not to focus on doing the do?"

Now, if you haven't already considered me strange, you may think so after you read the following: One of my secrets in maintaining a healthy purity journey is by talking to God regularly about sex, even when I am really craving to have physical pleasure!

In other words, when I am aroused, I reach out to God.

As I shared with you in Chapter 1, 'We need God's help to maintain purity.' One of the ways for you and I to do just that is to be in regular and transparent communication with God.

Spoiler alert! He already knows what we are feeling.

Sexual triggers will not go away the moment you decide to announce you are choosing purity. In fact, the longer you are practicing abstinence or celibacy in your singleness the more sexual triggers you will experience.

I believe sexual triggers increase the further you are along in your purity journey for you to learn exactly how to rely on God's strength and not your own. Because let's face it, if you could have gotten purity right on your own by now, would you really be reading this book?

For this reason, the sooner you invite God by asking him what to do whenever you experience a sexual trigger the better your process will be! I'm sure this may be hard for you to imagine, so let me share with you some more Biblical knowledge found in James 1:5.

'If you need wisdom, ask our generous God and He will give it to you. And He won't rebuke you for asking!'

This scripture is beneficial for you to know no matter what sexual trigger you may face God can provide you with a solution without condemnation. God loves you so much that his line of communication is always open! (Remember, Psalms 46:1)

He is not going to hit ignore because you need His help yet again in managing your sexual desires. In fact, this bring me to one of the most valuable Nuggets in handling sexual urges!

Get your notebook and pen ready because this may become your new mantra:

There is no sexual trigger God cannot defuse.

Was this a shock to you? Now, you may have noticed that I rephrased this Nugget for you. The reason is that I really want you to understand your sexual urges are powerful.

However, there is divine assistance available whenever you are ready to disable any sexual trigger from causing damage to your purity. You don't have to wait until after you have succumbed or set off a sexual trigger. Learn from Eve!

All you have to say is one name, Jesus, and he will provide everything you need. Okay, let me really break down this Nugget for you.

When you get hot and bothered, you can ask God to help you to remain pure, not Netflix & Chill! If you can't sleep at night, there's no need to masturbate, you can pray to God for peace!

If you are having flashbacks of a sexual encounter, you don't have to look up pornography, you can ask God to help you to overcome temptation. Honey Bunches, I am going after this hard with you because I want you to understand with divine assistance, it is possible to manage all sexual triggers.

No matter how big or small God can provide you with the know-how on overcoming any sexual trigger that may appear in your single season! For example, when you were a child, how did you learn the proper way take a bath?

How did you know how to turn on the water, set the temperature of the water, lather the soap, and rinse off?

How did you become aware of the times you need to practice this form of hygiene?

Did you have an epiphany during recess in kindergarten to simply do those things on your own? Or, did someone show you how?

Now, of course, the answer is simple: someone taught you! You didn't just wake up one day knowing how to properly maintain cleanliness.

More than likely, an adult like your parents, guardians, or even your siblings gave you the wisdom. And, you may have even asked a lot of questions throughout the process like,

"Will I go down the drain when I take out the stopper?" Maybe, that was just me!

In the same way of you needing guidance to practice cleanliness then you will now need wisdom from a reliable source to help you manage sex in your singleness. Once again, you cannot maintain purity on your own!

To be truly successful and confident along your journey is through the wisdom of our creator, God. With your permission only, He will guide you to escape even the most intense sexual temptations! (1 Corinthians 10:13)

Now, I want to warn you, sexual temptations no matter if you choose abstinence or celibacy the journey will be difficult! Therefore, it is important for you to have the right support! For the next few pages, I will share exactly how you can successfully manage them both!

Did you really think I would leave you out of the loop?

Aht! Aht! Now, it's time to get into the nitty gritty!

Handling Sexual Temptations In Purity

By being exposed to pornography so early in life, I had experienced countless cycles of going back to The Affair that hypnotically pulled me into its grasp. Many doors of perversion opened up for me and I walked through to fulfill any sexual craving, unknowingly how to stop.

I'd tried with every ounce in me to avoid looking at porn, stop answering calls/texts to "come chill", stop depending on masturbation to help me sleep at night, and stop believing my sex could "make someone keep coming back to me".

When I first chose purity, I decided to take the celibacy route. After everything I had been through, I was so spiritually broken and frankly was desperate for a change!

I relied on my relationship with The Affair for so long that when I made the decision to choose celibacy, I felt like a person going through a spiritual rehab! Every day without some form of engagement in sexual pleasure my body went through withdrawals.

My mind would battle with thoughts of past sexual experiences or images I'd encountered.

It didn't matter if I was awake, sleep, or a part of a conversation with someone the urge to have sex consumed me. It was like I could not shake the impulse!

I felt completely disgusted with myself. I didn't understand why I wasn't able on my own to "kick the habit".

Does this sound familiar to you and your purity journey?

If so, let me share how you, too, can gain control over sexual triggers in purity. Now, if you haven't experienced any of the above while being involved with The Affair, good for you.

However, take notes! It can happen to you!

You see, my first attempt at purity didn't last long. As a result, it took me failing many times throughout the years, to finally "get it right" where I chose to seek God and trust His way on managing sex in my singleness!

And, this is what I desire to help you avoid and overcome. What helped to transform my mind in celibacy and what I want you to learn in your purity journey is that we must receive The Holy Spirit as an aide.

The Holy Spirit will help reveal things to you that you never knew existed! For me, by having a spiritual connection, I was able to discover a hidden truth that did not appear to me in previous attempts in purity.

This can only happen for you in your purity journey if you allow the Holy Spirit to guide you. How you can do this is by inviting The Holy Spirit to be your aide!

You can simply say, "Holy Spirit, I give you permission to lead me."

Now, you may also wonder what was the hidden truth that The Holy Spirit revealed to me in celibacy. Don't worry, I got you!

Sexual triggers in purity tend to thrive off one's own mental emotions.

'Temptation comes from our own desires, which entice us and drag us away." -James 1:14

Like any other temptation, for every sexual trigger you face in purity tends to start in your own mind.

Sorry, Honey Bunches! The devil doesn't always make you do it!

Meaning, sexual triggers are created by your own imagination, not solely through the temptation of other people or even Satan. Therefore, it is important for you to be in control of what you allow inside of your mind!

For example, have you ever spent time listening to songs with lyrics that are sexually suggestive? Or have you watched a movie with intense sexual scenes?

Think about how you felt in those moments. Physically? Mentally?

If you are anything like me, I am sure either:

A. You think about a past sexual experience.

Or

B. You think about wanting to have a sexual experience.

Believe it or not, your mind is powerful! Whatever is inside your mind has the potential to push you toward what you desire.

In purity, this is where The Holy Spirit comes in handy! When you are faced with a sexual trigger, I believe The Holy Spirt tries to intervene and help you from being victimized by The Affair! Let's go back to the example of watching a movie.

Have you ever wanted to watch a certain movie on Netflix, but you notice its rating is TV-MA? Immediately, you check to see why and discover the movie has strong sexual content and language!

Though you sense the urge to change from viewing the movie and find something else to watch, you brush it off due to you really wanting to view.

After a while, you notice while viewing or after watching, certain sexual scenes turned you on physically. You may have even felt slightly guilty for watching the movie in the first place. I want you to know that 'initial feeling' for you to not watch the film was the Holy Spirit!

You see, the Holy Spirit doesn't speak on His own; he will guide you into all truth. He will even warn you of things you should or shouldn't do that will impact your future. (John 16:13)

A great future in purity is attached to the Holy Spirit.

In fact, there are three simple truths I believe for you becoming a warrior in successfully managing purity: Be Aware of Your Sexual Triggers, Listen When The Holy Spirit Is Speaking To You, and Set Boundaries To Prevent Engaging In Sexual Sin & Stick To Them!

I believe by practicing these key components throughout your purity journey will help you to win in purity. For the final pages of this section, I will share with you how to apply these purity concepts for you to do just that!

Be Aware of Your Sexual Triggers

Being aware of your sexual triggers is very important in whatever purity route you choose because you must understand what has the possibility to cause harm to your purity!

Honey Bunches, if you want to overcome The Affair you cannot afford to be attempting this process all 'willy nilly'. Remember your purity is your gold. The moment you chose purity you officially joined a battle, a battle for your gold! Like any battle, you have things to try and cause you to stumble. You see, your purity season is not limited to focusing on not having sex.

If you do not already know, it is time! It is time for you to know what triggers you, sexually.

What causes you to watch pornography?
Is it having difficulty sleeping?
Why do you choose to answer late night calls from the person who repeatedly causes harm towards your purity?
Can you not change your number or block theirs from calling you?

What causes you to masturbate?
Is it boredom?

What is triggering you to be involved with The Affair?

Now, I gave you a few examples. However, your sexual triggers may differ. No sexual trigger is greater than another.

What is important is for you to acknowledge what causes you to want to be with The Affair.

How about you try it out now!

On the following page, I created a space for you to make a list of your sexual triggers. Jot down all the things that you believe triggers you to engage with The Affair.

My Sexual Triggers

Good job! Since you are aware of the thing(s) causing damage to your purity, I want to be one of the first people to congratulate you because you just took a huge step that most people do not like to do: admitting you need help.

Let me share with you how you can receive what you need:

Listen When the Holy Spirit is Speaking To You

By all means the more you are in tuned with the word of God the Holy Spirit will be dropping small Nuggets in your spirit that will make you go "Something told me not to…"

Yet, it is only up to you to listen to His voice! How can you hear it? Honey Bunches, you got to dig deep… in the word of God of course.

The more you dig deeper in the word of God the more your spiritual ears will open and be in tuned when you are experiencing those hot and heavy moments!

Making a routine to be in the word of God will reset and refocus you in wisdom and away from all tactics of the enemy in trying to sever your purity journey. You have to be intentional in protecting your mindset every day!

> "But they delight in the law of the Lord, meditating on it day and night. They are like trees planted along the riverbank, bearing fruit each season. Their leaves never wither, and they prosper in all they do." Psalms 1:2-3

The more you are spending time in the word of God, the stronger your mind will be to handle any sexual trigger.

It doesn't matter if you have been practicing abstinence or celibacy starting today, a week, a month, one year, or ten plus years hiding yourself in the word of God regularly is where the Holy Spirit speaks to and encourages you.

Early in my purity journey, each day that I went without sex or masturbation was a victory for me! By daily submitting to read God's word, saying the simple prayer, "God, help me to manage my sexual desires.", listening to that 'something told me voice' aka The Holy Spirit, was a superb dosage I discovered spiritually to avoid going back to The Affair.

Honey Bunches, I would hide myself so much in God's word, you would have thought I was on salary for the Lord! In reality, I was filling up my mind to understand how to acknowledge the voice of God.

The enemy would try to feed me lies about how silly I was and try to convince me I was missing out from what everyone was doing. Yet, the more I relied on God's wisdom through the Holy Spirit I learned all that I needed to avoid The Affair.

What I am not saying is you need to drown yourself in God's word in order to understand The Holy Spirit! However, choose to find time to gain a relationship with God (by seeking God) to know His voice.

In purity, you will have many feelings. You may desire to go somewhere and all of a sudden become overwhelm with 'a feeling' to stay home. Don't silence The Holy Spirit inside of you. He speaks. Listen.

Listening to The Holy Spirit when he speaks to you will help you conquer the daily battle with The Affair, even minor pitfalls you didn't see coming.

God's word also states, "my sheep know my voice!" In order for you to do just that, it is going to take you being intentional.

Are you up for the challenge?

Set Boundaries To Prevent Engaging In Sexual Triggers & Stick To Them!

Think about it! Have you ever been sexually active while being single (not married) and enjoyed the full experience? I know I haven't!

If you have ever acted in sex or masturbation, you know the experience doesn't end in climax. It's the moment after in what solidifies the full sexual experience!

During this time, it is where you may think about what just took place. And, when you're single, this is the time I believe the Holy Spirit tries to intervene by helping you to not fall victim to do what you just did, again!

Let me explain further for you to get what I'm saying. No matter how amazing the pleasure may feel in the moment it is the after experience where you will have a tiny significance in "second guessing" your own actions!

I believe this helps to understand having sex outside of marriage or participating in masturbation is not natural when you feel bad for "doing it".

Right when you're all cuddled up with your Bae/Boo/Friend with Benefits/Entanglement Partner OR right when you given your big sigh of relief from receiving pleasure, doesn't there always seem to be a slight tug at your heart of guilt?

No matter if you are a believer or non-believer, I am confident guilt will come across your mind on what you did. Making you wonder, "Should I have done that?" or say quietly, "Okay, this will be the last time."

Do you remember the first Nugget I shared in Chapter 2: Being strong in purity comes by you being fully dependent on God?

You can brush away the thought to be sexual, yet it disappears temporarily until the next encounter. This is why maintaining purity is something that's hard to undergo without God's assistance. It's simply impossible!

Some people would say having sex is natural for human beings to enjoy regularly. And I couldn't agree more! But, it is best for us to be under the covenant of God, marriage, to fully enjoy sex.

If you can admit, any time you've been sexual, or participated in The Affair, you eventually regretted your decision. As a result, you felt victimized or embarrassed by being involved with The Affair in the first place!

Therefore, you couldn't allow yourself to leave The Affair though the relationship was damaging. I was there too.

Over two decades, my involvement with The Affair led me to accepting its traits as a way of affection and bliss though our encounters only lasted for split moments with no complete pleasure.

With The Affair, I never had contentment. The satisfaction I craved fell short of one hundred percent!

For every involvement with The Affair, lead to the aftermath of a conviction so strong in the heart that I would tell myself, "This is going to be the last time". Knowing I wasn't ready to let go!

As you may know, when engaging with The Affair, it is not something to enjoy just one time. It is like ice cream!

If you have a moment with it, you want to have it again and again and again. This is why it is not only important to be aware of your sexual triggers and listen to The Holy Spirit in hot and heavy moments.

Setting boundaries and sticking to them is a way you can be proactive in applying what the Holy Spirit is saying to you!

Setting boundaries and sticking to them helps you to not engage to any form of sexual sin which is just as important!

Therefore, I want to help you to set those necessary boundaries for you to avoid The Affair.

Let's use the example of Netflix again.

Say you are wanting to get a brand new account for you and a small child. Imagine the child is your own and is about three years old.

Once you set up your account, you notice you have the ability to create separate profiles within the account. You choose to move forward with individual profiles due to you and the child's preferences in what you all want to watch.

Now, are you going to allow the child to have a similar profile as you? Of course, not!

More than likely, you will set certain parental guard to prevent the child from going to certain shows or movies. Just in case, they accidentally stumble upon something that has the potential to expose them to what they are not mature enough to handle.

Similar to you and your heavenly Father, God. Right now, there are specific sexual desires available to you. However, when God created you in His image, He knew the desires you would have.

That is why I believe He created marriage to place as a 'parental guard' to protect you in your singleness until you are ready for marriage and able to handle all that comes with sex.

When you choose to set boundaries and stick to them in purity, it is a way to help you avoid falling victim to The Affair.

The first way of going about setting boundaries and sticking to them in purity is pretty literal: Set boundaries.

For example, you may have to make the decision to no longer masturbate because when you masturbate you are heightening the desire to be sexual.

You may have to choose to quit pornography cold turkey. Because when you are looking at those images and listen to those people on those movies you are triggering your sexual desires!

You may have to set certain parental guards on your smart devices such as your phone, laptop, or television.

You may also have to ask your intentional accountability to set passwords for you on certain devices, so you can no longer have access with The Affair.

Now, I am simply sharing some of the boundaries I had to move forward to overcome The Affair. The boundaries you set up may look a lot different.

Do you remember the sexual trigger list you created a few pages back? Now, let's put this list into an even better use. For every sexual trigger you listed on the page, set a boundary for you to not engage.

The goal is for you to be proactive to set up guards to not engage with The Affair. I'll share with you examples on the following page.

Then, complete one for your personal use.

My Boundaries

Examples:

No calls after 11PM:
There's something about late night calls that seems to invite freaky convos.

No visits with significant others while home alone: I am tempted to get physical.

Have my intentional accountability know about every step I take in dating: I need a Godly community to remain committed to my purity journey.

No Kissing...below the lips! :) : Kissing below the lips can tempt me or my significant other to desire to be more physical.

No Porn: I get aroused when watching.

No Masturbation: I am tempted to be sexual with someone else whenever I masturbate.

My Boundaries

Now, it is your turn! You may use the examples I listed on the previous page or create your own. Use the lines below to create your boundaries list.

_____

_____

_____

_____

_____

_____

_____

You are stronger than your sexual desires.

I understand how hard that may have been for you. Remember, I am just like you. I have been where you are!

Another reason how The Affair can keep you coming back is due to not fully turning over all sexual desires to God.

Therefore, in order for you to do just that is by establishing and keeping healthy purity boundaries. You can try to beg God to simply take away your sexual urges. However, God doesn't work that way!

What I mean is God will not force Himself into your situations. He is a gentleman; it is not a part of His character!

To emphasize Romans 9:19 says,

"Well then, you might say, why does God blame people for not responding? Haven't they simply done what He makes them do? Further down, the Bible gives us the answer in verse 22, "In the same way, even though God has the right to show His anger and His power, He is very patient with those on whom His anger falls, who are destined for destruction."

Although God has the power, Romans 9 gives the perfect explanation that you, Honey Bunches, are free to make our own decisions without being forced by God!

Maybe you're like me and wish at times God could still press a "pause button" on all your sexual desires until you get married.

The good news is though, you cannot be controlled by God to stop acting on your sexual emotions. He can be patient enough to wait on you to make the decision.

God loves you so much that when He created you, He gave you The Holy Spirit to decipher what's right from what's wrong.

Establish Your Boundaries.

Rely on your heavenly assistance.

Release your control!

Sex Nuggets

What Thought(s) Comes To Mind After Engaging In The Affair?

_____

_____

_____

_____

_____

_____

_____

❦Sex Nuggets❦

How Do You Feel Being Involved With The Affair vs Maintaining Purity?

_____

_____

_____

_____

_____

_____

_____

_____

II. How To Sustain Joy In Purity

Chapter 5

There's not one person who can be you the way that you are.

I cannot think of one moment in my life where I haven't been competitive. If I can remember correctly, the joy of winning sparked within me through watching my family as a child.

My family starts off with my two parental units (Momma and Daddy). Then, I have three older brothers and a sister. We also have a god sister as well who's close within our family unit.

I am the youngest of my parent's children and we are all about five years a part in age. Meaning, I had and have great opportunity to watch and learn from my family, especially my older siblings!

Now, every person in my family is unique in their own way. Seriously, everyone has their opinions and minds to be themselves.

However, there are two distinct things about my family members where I believe they each have in common: they love games and they love to win them!

Till this day, there is not a holiday where the game of football, basketball, tennis, or even Family Feud is not blaring loudly from a tv's speakers! Throughout the time, you will find my competitive parents and siblings surrounding (or sometimes hovering) near a tv cheering and shouting at who's ever competing in hopes their favorite team(s) will win.

While growing up in my parent's home, being a competitor was the norm! Quite often, my parents hosted card games for our family and friends of the family to play. Even my older siblings all played some type of sport or was a part of a team.

And, anyone who joined there was no room for quitting!
My father would often say, 'If you do something, do it to the best of your ability.'

As the youngest, I was practically everyone in my family's tiny cheerleader. Literally! Back then, you would find me somewhere within bleachers, benches or along school gymnasium's sidelines cheering on for my older siblings' school teams with cheer chants.

Likewise, I even recalled a period of my life as an actual mascot cheerleader for my older sister's cheer squad. Honey Bunches, you couldn't tell me nothing!

By encouraging my family to dominate in games, it birthed the thrill of winning within me! Therefore, no matter the game I play in life, I play with the mindset to always win.

Now, you can judge me or my family all you want, however, I must ask you, 'How often have you treated your purity process this way?' 'When is the last time you competed against something during your process?' And if you don't believe you have, let's ask one of the things you choose to compete with almost every day: Time.

Time isn't your competitor...the enemy is.

You may already know Satan is your enemy or competitor in your spiritual journey. (John 10:10) Like Satan, I believe time can become one of the biggest competitors in your purity process as well!

Time can be a bit tricky and without warning, time has the ability to deter you away from your purity in two distinct ways which are the following: Being Too Focused On Time In Purity or Overly Comparing Your Time In Purity.

At any moment you allow time to be your motivation in purity, your journey will no longer be moving forward in purpose, yet driven by the ambition of time.

One of the best ways you can know if time is your competitor is to be aware of how you treat time during this season! Therefore, I want to help you avoid the traps of time if you're just starting purity or help you get out of time's traps if you've been stuck while overcoming The Affair.

Let's start by tackling the first topic together, Being Too Focused On Time In Purity by you answering the following:

During your time in purity, how many times have you shared that you have gone without sex or masturbation this month?

        A. 1 to 3 Times
        B. 4 to 6Times
        C. 7 to 9Times
        D. 10 or More Times

Now, if today is your first day in purity, you don't have to answer. However, I encourage you to continue reading this chapter because I believe you will need to hear what I am about to say.

The above answers B. C. or D. are not the best ways I encourage you of going forward in purity. Therefore, if you chose those answers, I want to share with you why and how to help you to shift your focus on winning against your real competitor in purity, Satan!

One strategy I learned early on in overcoming The Affair was to not be too focus on the amount of time I had been without sex and masturbation. In previous attempts, any time I would discuss or celebrate my time away from sex, not too soon after I would find myself going back to The Affair.

I would listen to well-known social media influencers who shared a similar journey as me and would be extremely fixated on arriving towards their same destinations such as 1 month of No Sex…6 Months of No Sex…or even 1 Year of No Sex.

What I didn't realize then I was subconsciously competing against their time! As a result, I placed unnecessary pressure to perform a process that was only intended for someone else which led me to discontentment.

For this reason, I repeatedly failed at purity because my focus was limited to the amount of time I had been in purity hoping I could get to their certain 'purity point' or even surpass it!

This way of thinking kicked my entire behind! Truth be told at that time The Affair wore me out like the Boston Celtics did the Los Angeles Lakers in the 2008 NBA Finals. No Cap!

All things considered, this is why I believe being too focused on time in purity will only prolong your journey! If you are ever more focused on a specific time being in purity or constantly talking about reaching a certain time in purity, I guarantee your process will only lasts as long or not too soon after that time has occurred.

Here is what to look for! The first sign if you are being too focused on time in purity is you are constantly talking about your time in purity. This can be pretty simple to detect!

Pay attention to your conversations with your friends, family, or even strangers. Are you mostly talking about how long it's been without you having sex?

Even if the starting topic is about something totally different like work, or finding something to eat, do you somehow share an update of you not participating in masturbation?

I understand sometimes it can be difficult to find fault in your own self, you know because you are so amazing! Therefore, I have one other way you can see if you are competing against time....Ask.

On the contrary, I am not saying to ask that stranger you may have shared your purity journey to. I am referring to your intentional accountability.

You know those persons who are intentional to hold you accountable to your purity process! If their response to your question is somewhere along the lines of "Yeah", "Yes" or "Well...you know you do seem a bit passionate about" Then, Honey Bunches you have your answer.

When you have discovered you are too focused on time in purity the next step is for you to shift your focus back to Your Why! Remember, Your Why is what helps you to keep going strong in purity.

Hear me out. I do believe you should be proud of yourself on overcoming The Affair. Every step you take away from sex or masturbation in your singleness is one worth celebrating!

On the other hand, never be so focused on the amount of time being without The Affair that you lose sight of Your Why to start in the first place.

Now, let's talk about who you should focus on winning against, Satan.

Stay alert! Watch out for your great enemy, the devil. "He prowls around like a roaring lion, looking for someone to devour." - 1 Peter 5:8

Your competitor in purity is the devil, Satan. He desires to get you off focused from what God has planned for you.

Satan's methods do not change. His purpose is to steal, kill, and destroy.

If he can keep you distracted or cause you to give up on this season of purity, he will feel like he's won. Do not allow Satan to shift your focus!

In the words of my father, "There are no vacation days in being a Christian." Make sure you are always on guard because the enemy is waiting for any opportunity to cause you to slip up or lose hope.

The good news is that you are never alone in overcoming Satan's tactics to try and lead you to The Affair.

Just how your competitor, the enemy, has his daily mission, you my friend have something greater, Jesus. Jesus came that you might have life and life to the full. (John 10:10)

You already have victory in Jesus to win against Satan. You also have The Holy Spirit and God's word to help you. Be intentional with all!

Your purity process is not a death sentence!

Be honest. Choosing a season of abstinence or celibacy will sometimes make you feel like it's going to last for..e'..ver! (Yes, that was definitely a reference to The Sandlot!)

I believe this occurs when you overly compare your time in purity. Therefore, your process will feel like the end of the world.

You may notice you experience these feeling when you see others achieving certain things you desire such as success, marriage, children, or you fill in the blank!

Your purity journey is a lifestyle to honor God with your body, heart, mind, and spirit. Meaning, any time you are comparing where you are to someone else's process, time has become your competitor in your purity.

The goal in purity is for you to sustain joy in the decision you made, not simply bear the process to others. You can do this by keeping in mind you are in a season of purity. And, every season has an expiration date!

"For everything there is a season, a time for every activity under heaven." -Ecclesiastes 3:1

Your season in purity will not be like anyone else's season. Therefore, what you experience during this time will be for you to grow stronger in who God's called you to be.

Besides, who else can be you the way that you are?

Galatians 6:4 says it best, "Pay careful attention to your own work, for then you will get the satisfaction of a job well done, and you won't need to compare yourself to anyone else."
Or, like the saying goes "Comparison is the thief of all joy"!

To put this differently, don't allow anything to steal your joy in this amazing decision you have made, including time.

Similar to last chapter's sexual triggers list, I believe it is just as important to be aware of comparison triggers. Meaning, you should be aware of what is encouraging you to compare your season to someone else's.

Let's take a pause right here for you to do just that. Write down the thing(s) that is causing you to compare your time in purity:

_____

_____

_____

_____

Look at you! Now, you're on a roll. For everything that is on the list above I want you to pray to God asking Him to help heal you from comparing yourself to what you just shared.

For example, let's say you wrote social media on your list. You can say, 'God, thank you for allowing me to have access to social media. However, I ask for you to help me to no longer compare my journey with what I see in others on social media. May you heal me from comparison and help me to grow purposeful connections through social media,
Amen.
Continue this process until you have prayed for everything that is on your list. You'll be surprised by how your perception changes with God's help towards people and things.

Yes, the wait may hurt. Waiting is never fun, but trust in Jesus. Because of your obedience, I believe He has greater for you.

Believe the promise will be worth the process.

❧Waiting Nuggets❧

What if God's plan is for you to be in purity longer than you expected? How do you plan to move forward in your purity process?

_____

_____

_____

_____

_____

_____

_____

🐦Waiting Nuggets🐦

In this chapter, you made a 'Comparison Trigger List' and were to pray over your list. Take a step further and share your list with your intentional accountability. Ask them to pray over your list too!

_____

_____

_____

_____

_____

_____

_____

_____

Chapter 6

You are not obligated to answer to your past.

When I became serious about overcoming The Affair, I had to let go of perceptions I carried from my past. This included how I viewed myself! I began to understand who I wanted to be and in order for me to walk in that boldly I had to face reality.

Everything I allowed to control me I felt was attached by a cord of lies someone had spoken over me that I had accepted. Criticism. The sly jokes of me not being valuable because I had already been involved in sex.

Fear. Anxious thoughts that no one would ever love me, 'the real me' because of my body count.

I had to make a decision to no longer allow anyone's negative spoken words, including my very own, to rule over me. It was like I could physically feel my breakthrough at the tips of my fingers.

At the same time, there was a force so strong trying to pull me back to what I had outgrew. Doubt, lies, and self-condemnation all played a horrific symphony in my mind and the tune didn't stop until I surrendered who I was is no longer who I am.

In purity, there is going to be a time or times where you will have to face the p word: your past. You cannot afford to do things the same way; the health of your purity is going to require you to do things differently!

"Therefore, if any man be in Christ, he is a new creature: old things are passed away; behold, all things are become new."
-2 Corinthians 5:17

Once you have accepted Christ and have given Him your heart, you no longer have to hold on to the person that you once were. Even the very actions you involved yourself with, Christ has forgiven you for.

So, why not extend that same grace to yourself?

In particular, when I made the decision to surrender my life to Christ and started to be intentional in my new purity journey. I made a decision to stop answering to my past, including a nickname that was given to me 'Bre'. Growing up I thought it was so cool to have other people call me Bre.

However, the more I moved forward away from The Affair, God began to reveal to me my true identity in Him. This led me to gain understanding on even the tiniest of details about myself including the meaning of my actual name, Breonna, which means strength.

In the midst of that revelation, I grew confidence in not settling to answer when people call me 'Bre'. Why is this, you ask? In the words of Tyler Perry, 'It ain't what people call you. It's what you answer to.'

If my name is strength, why would I choose to accept part of it when God has called me to more? Therefore, I now prefer to be called Breonna or by my current initials BG, (which ironically, I read somewhere the letters B G mean House of God in Hebrew).

Believe it or not making the decision to stop answering to my former name has been a mental healing process within itself. Speaking of healing mentally, let's talk about what's on your mind!

'To be lost in your thoughts is a very very complex art and the things that you find are surprising. It's the way you believe that becomes the very things you see.'
-Janelle Monae

Let's be clear the enemy doesn't want you to have a successful purity journey! One main way I believe the enemy tries to get you off focus is mentally.

Therefore, he will try to distract you with many lies and attempts to end your purity by reminding you of your past failures. His goal is to make you feel vulnerable enough to give in to your sexual triggers and steal your purity by simply causing you to give up even pursuing it!

No matter how weak or strong you think you are in purity it is his daily mission for you to give into how you feel and ignore what you know is true. You will experience low moments in purity.

Your sexual triggers will not vanish simply by you choosing to commit to a season of purity! The way you prosper in purity is by taking control of your mind.

After being without The Affair for a period of time, your past will knock at your door whether by a person or memory. Having the right mindset will sustain you in purity. PERIOD.

Think about anything you have had to overcome or learn. In order for you to accomplish what you desired it was necessary for your mind to be focused, right? That's the same with purity!

You have to be in control of your thoughts and what you choose to be protective of is what has your focus. If not, your thoughts will consume you.

As you read in Chapter 4, it's hard to focus on purity by listening to music with explicit language or words overly being sexualized! Likewise, it's hard to watch movies with strong sexual scenes or even engaging in conversations with someone who keeps pushing the topic of sex.

The reason is simple it heightens your sexual desires! Regardless of your past, during your purity it's a fresh start for you to be pure. Pure in your heart. Pure in your mind. Pure in your spirit!

Honey Bunches, as a child of God, you are called to be apart of the world, not of it. (Philippians 4:8)

The best way to get revenge over your past is to move forward in purpose.

Now, we've talked about your past, let's talk about how you can move forward within your present and future in purity!

Have you ever noticed after being involved with The Affair the amount of time you spent will periodically cross your mind? You may wish you could get time back due to guilt or other reasons that are more valuable than a few minutes of pleasure.

I shared a little with you last chapter about how to not compete against time. In this chapter, I would also like to share with you how to steward well over your time in purity by making use of the thing you were gifted with: your gift.

Yes, you have a gift.
You see when you were born, you were given a gift. And, I'm not referring to the balloons, clothes, and teddy bears at your birthing hospital. Before you entered this world, your first gift was purpose. (Jeremiah 1:5)

In fact, I want you to say that out loud. 'I have a gift.' Say it again, but say it loud enough to make the person who may be sitting next to you believes it too. 'I have a gift!'

When God created you, He created you on purpose. Now, that purpose can only be discovered by you through Him. With this in mind, ask yourself what do you enjoy, yet challenges you, and helps others?
Is it cooking? Writing? Singing? Encouraging others?

Whatever it is, taking time to use your gift in singleness I believe is the best time you should start being intentional with your gift! Here's why.

Your Gift Will Make Room For You.

"A man's gift [given in love or courtesy] makes room for him and brings him before great men." -Proverbs 18:16 AMP

You were not created to be average. The very gift God has given you is for you to use to help others, so God can get the glory through you.

How Does This Look?

Spend time every day doing the following:

Reading The Bible:
'The Bible exists to help us to thrive.'
The Holy Spirit:
'The Holy Spirt is one the greatest assets in your life.'

Invest In Your Gift:
'Your assignment requires investment.'

Shoutout to Dr. Dharius Daniels once again for the above excerpts! (YouTube The Bible Detox..Then, thank me later!)

When you are using your gift, it is going to help you move forward in what you were created to do!

Make the decision to move forward only accepting the words of The One, who is the author of your life's journey, not what you have overcome.

I say all this to say the more you are away from The Affair you will learn the benefits of the time you have and the importance of managing that time you have wisely.

You are chosen. Use Your Gift!

Purpose Nuggets

What thought patterns would you like for God to help you to heal?

_____

_____

_____

_____

_____

_____

_____

🐦Purpose Nuggets🐦

Time cannot heal all your wounds, God does! How will you plan to move forward in purpose to thrive in your purity season? (Ex. Counseling, Therapy, etc.)

_____

_____

_____

_____

_____

_____

_____

_____

Chapter 7

Success is using mistakes and developing them into lessons.

Uh-oh! Let's talk about it. You know. Slip ups. Whether you are choosing to take the abstinence or celibacy route, slip ups can happen. And, if they happen, it can feel like the worst!

You may feel defeated, even worthless. And, as soon as it happens, that is when the enemy begins to fill your mind with all kinds of lies such as:

'God doesn't love you.'

'You failed too big that God will not forgive you.'

Or, 'You should just keep doing what you are doing since you've already done it.'

Out of all the billions of people who are living or lived in the world we all have one thing in common: we all have made mistakes! That's right, even Queen Bey! Feel better?

Basically, there is not one person who hasn't messed up which is a beautiful thing about life, noone is perfect!

"For everyone has sinned; we all fall short of God's glorious standard." -Romans 3:23

With this in mind, there may come a point in your journey where you may make the mistake by giving into The Affair.

You may find yourself going back to a pornographic site or engage sexually. That doesn't mean you have to continue to be entangled with The Affair! Instead, you have the opportunity to learn from where you went wrong.

Honey Bunches, you cannot fail too big that God will not forgive you! Therefore, for this entire chapter, I am going to share with you two helpful steps that you can use to bounce back to purity, if you have fallen victim to The Affair.

Repent/Turn Away From/Do A 180!

When you have made the decision to engage with The Affair, your first step is to repent. All repenting means is to ask God for forgiveness and turn away from the thing that caught you slipping. (Acts 3:19 and Acts 26:18)

Or, what I like to call 'Do A 180!' When you Do A 180!, this means for you to run as far as you can in the opposite direction from whatever triggered you sexually.

As can be seen in 1 Corinthians 6:18, to Do A 180! is quite beneficial for you in your purity! This scripture states:

"Run from sexual sin! No other sin so clearly affects the body as this one does. For sexual immorality is a sin against your own body."

Now, I know what you are thinking.

How can I run away from sexual sin when I don't even like running during cardio!
Running from sexual sin is a heart's decision for you to surrender your sexual desires back to God after engaging with The Affair.

Then, you will be encouraged to take progressive steps (like running) back to your purity process.

So, there is no need to worry about getting a personal trainer!

When you have made the decision to repent, it is where you can also seek God and ask for Him to give you wisdom to say no to The Affair. In addition, once you have repented be prepared to experience more chances for you to turn away from The Affair.

Meaning, when you turn away from sexual sin and ask God for His guidance and wisdom, He's not going to be like 'Poof! Here's wisdom!' In fact, I believe you will experience more opportunities for you to learn how to say no to engage in sexual sin.

These Do A 180! opportunities come from God because He loves you and wants the best for you, and He's not trying to put something along your path for you to fail.

My belief is that God does this so you can learn from what you have experienced. Kinda like good parents!

Good parents will make sure their child or children has all the right things they need to be in successful life. Often, good parents will help their children receive this information by sharing it with them, especially during times where the child has made a mistake.

For example, I remember my mom sharing a story with me about a good parent, a child and a hot stove. Apparently, the good parent shared with the child not to touch the stove because the stove was hot.

Well, the child didn't understand the definition of hot and wanted to touch the stove anyway. Hence, the child made the decision to touch the stove and got burned!

In the light of this story, can you see where I am going?

God is like a good parent. When you are placed in attractive situations that may cause harm to you, He is going to try to protect you through The Holy Spirit, so you will not get burned.

What is causing you to engage?

After you have made a decision to Repent/ Turn Away From/ Do A 180!, your next step is to see where you went wrong by evaluating your actions to engage.

Was it by watching a certain tv series or movie? Were you listening to a specific music artist?

Who was around you? What did your environment look like when you engaged with The Affair? Were you experiencing boredom or having difficulty sleeping?

If I can be even more transparent, one of the most notorious places where I used to engage with The Affair was the bed. That's probably a pretty obvious response, right?

Beds are comfortable and available, especially with The Affair! While lying in the bed late night or early in the morning, it was there where flashbacks from past sexual experiences appeared casually in my mind.

Similarly, I noticed by being in the bed this phenomenon would continue until I moved around or got away from the environment I was in!

By me physically getting out of the bed, it was like I was making the decision to spiritually run away from what was causing me to engage with The Affair. Honey Bunches, sometimes, you got to move around!

Find that place of escape where you can go and pray to God to help you in hot moments. I get it. And, I know what you are probably thinking.

I am making this sound a lot easier than what you may have experienced! Running away may not always be as easy as I am sharing, but I want to let you know one more thing.

In the word of God it says, "God always gives you a way of escape He will not tempt you beyond what you can handle." (1 Corinthians 10:13)

The next time you are having a moment of strong sexual temptation and you are really trying to be strong in your purity remove yourself from the environment that you are in and allow the Holy Spirit to assist you and I guarantee He will do just that!

❧Healing Nuggets❧

No is one perfect. Slip-ups can sometimes occur in purity! What helpful tips shared in this chapter would you like to use in the case of slip-up in your purity?

_____

_____

_____

_____

_____

_____

_____

Healing Nuggets

1 Corinthians 10:13 lets you know God always gives a way of escape when facing The Affair. How do you find comfort knowing that God is willing to always come to your rescue?

_____
_____
_____
_____
_____
_____
_____

III. Being Bold & Confident In Purpose

Chapter 8

There's no good story untold.

With purity, I believe the more of us who choose to share in transparency will help the next generation and generations after to overcome The Affair. God heals us for His glory to bless others.

That's right! I don't believe this season you are going through is meant to stay hidden.

Every step you take away from The Affair, every tear you have cried, every close moment you thought about giving into temptation, I believe is not meant to be labeled as a simple "life lesson" or season.

Rather your journey has the ability to encourage someone else to overcome The Affair too!

Revelation 12:11 states, "...they overcome by the blood of the Lamb and the word of their testimony."

As embarrassing as my former addiction to pornography, masturbation, and sex is, I've found freedom and strength in Jesus by sharing with you the very things I've battled that God has help me to conquer.

Like me, I pray as you continue to move forward in your purity season and beyond that God will give you the wisdom and strength to help someone else along the way.

Do not let your testimony end with you.

Now, I am not saying for you to write a whole book and share your journey with the world! However, I do believe God will reveal to you how to share your story by using your gift.

Remember, no one can be you like you are!

Some of the greatest people in the world were chosen, like I believe you are, to do great things not because they were perfect, but they were obedient to God's calling over their lives.

In the same way, may you receive the boldness to live an extraordinary life in purpose while trusting God every step of the way. I pray God will begin to reveal the way he sees you to you.

As you continue to move forward in purity, let your light shine brightly. May every person see your light, so, they too, will come to know your Heavenly Father.

Bonus Section

To those who desire marriage in singleness,

Hold your breathe. Release. You got this!

Now, I'm sure many thoughts of doubt has crossed your mind at some point about choosing to surrender your sexuality to God. One thought in particular that used to really give me Jeepers Creepers was time.

Initially, I believed if God's plan for me was to have a lifetime of singleness I just knew it would only be for my good! I mean isn't that the beautiful thing about having faith in God: you don't know exactly how He will come through for you?

Like you, I made the decision to trust in God to provide me with anything I needed to handle.

Occasionally, I was reminded of long forgotten dreams of marriage. First, childhood memories would reappear in my mind about playing with Barbie dolls such as Ken and Barbie as a little girl.

Images of me sitting in the middle of my bedroom floor with my legs crossed. Barney wallpaper surrounding me as I made two dolls wed by pressing their faces together.

As soon as I would pull them a part, the following words I stated were, "You are now man and wife."

Throughout me daydreaming, I would find humor in my own impersonation of making my tiny voice go deep as I possibly could to sound like a traditional male Pastor. Then, a high-pitched giggle would escape out from my small frame.

I'd sigh nonchalantly while looking forward to the day I could be 'old enough' to become like Barbie. Then, I too, would be able to experience what my very own fairytale like Barbie and be with my husband, like Ken.

As time has passed, I've come a long way from those days playing with dolls. The idea of marriage will now come with an occasional question from a family member.

A random person may pull me to the side at a family dinner asking,

"When will you be getting married or having children?"
This question soon transitions with their beliefs of how I am approaching thirty and don't have much time left to be having kids.

Living in this purity season has taught me to truly depend on God's plan while sustaining joy in what is to come.

> *What if God's plan is for you to be in purity for a lifetime? Would you be up for the test?*

Do I see myself experiencing purity for a lifetime if that's God's design for my life? No, and I'll tell you why.

I believe in the Bible and I believe what the Bible says about the Bible.

And, according to Psalms 37:4, the Bible says, "to take delight in the Lord and he will give you the desires of your heart."
Since I am being faithful to God, He will not allow me to go through something I can't handle. *God, knows my needs!*

Therefore, I believe one day my season in marriage will happen in God's divine time.

While I wait, I plan to continue in freedom and joy because I believe God is going to blow my mind.
If marriage is something you really desire, I challenge you to take this moment right now to surrender your desires to God and take delight in Him.

Meaning, find joy with God, please God, be in an intentional relationship with God and I believe He will give you the desires of your heart, too!

Remember, you can ask God for any understanding, so ask God to help you manage your desires on marriage and pray for wisdom on how to move forward in joy while being pure.

God is faithful! In the Bible it also states, "He will never put more on us than we can bare." Remember, God loves you and He knows exactly what you need and when you need it! Because you have made the beautiful decision to choose purity, I believe He's going to absolutely blow your mind beyond your wildest dreams and expectations.

Choosing purity and waiting for marriage brings freedom from having to deal with self-condemnation of doing something you find pleasure in. Believe that everything works out for your good because you love God and you are called to His purpose.

You are not broken.

You are becoming.

Trust the process.

Acknowledgements

God.

I am who I am because of you. You see me beyond what I can imagine. Thank you for revealing to me the way you see me and giving me the courage to become her. With you, I believe you are helping me to be even better for the world to understand, with you all things are possible. Thank you for being everything that I need and more. This book cannot contain enough pages for me to give you the honor that you deserve. I would not have had the boldness, endurance, or words to empower if you weren't a part. This book is only completed because of you. God, I'm grateful you chose me. You promised, and you will never fail.

My Family.

Thank you for introducing me to God, love, and relationships. Your examples have given me tools to enhance the Kingdom of God and my future family. There's not one person who I love more. Thank you for your grace while I discovered and rediscovered the person who I needed to be. Most important, thank you all for being the best family ever, you are irreplaceable.

Seany Denson

I love you, BeFri. You see me at low and high moments. Yet, you provide the best version of yourself to enhance me. Thank you for being the right example to help me create the word: intentional accountability. You are the 'iron' that I need.

Acknowledgements

Sarah & Cam Bailey.
There is no other couple who I admire more. (Don't tell Momma & Daddy!) Your marriage has redefined love to me. Your journey inspires me to have an imperfect, yet progressing Godly marriage. Thank you for choosing me to be a student of your union and invest into my dreams. I am better because of you. I am better with you.

Genesis Holman.
Your very existence is divine. I don't believe I would have made my transition from The Affair to celibacy to abstinence without you. Thank you for always being the best person to keep me from going back to "The Affair". God's favor over you encourages me. I love you, Chica!

Shynette "Shy" Porter.
There are not enough words to describe our sisterhood. However, I couldn't imagine life without your love, support, and over all wittiness! You are valuable to me and I am forever grateful for you. Thank you.

Victoria Udebiuwa.
Girl, you are bomb.com! Thank you for being intentional in generosity. I've prayed for a friend like you, thank you for answering the call! I admire your strength and passion for words. Thank you for correcting me with grace.

Acknowledgements

Anna-Stacia Haley.
I'm sure this is a surprise to you! I honor you in my writing because you empowered me to finish strong. The day you sent me a copy of your book to "proofread" was the day I gained wisdom on how to finish my very own. Prophetess, thank you for being my Ram in The Bush. You are Heaven sent. May God continue to bless you in all you do!

Honey Bunches aka Empower Her Tribe.
Thank you for allowing me to lead and help strengthen you in your spiritual journeys. Every week, you invite the vision God gave me into your homes, jobs, schools, screens and etc. to empower. You challenge me to go deep into the presence of God daily and give my all in every work that is shared throughout our tribe. Your support is unmatched!

To My Soon to Be Life Partner.
Thank you for waiting with me. I haven't met you...yet. However, I believe we will soon meet in God's perfect timing and I am confident you are worth the wait :) May God continue to bless you in this season and beyond.

Acknowledgements

Anna Quarterson.

Thank you for being My Why. Your bold and transparent moment empowered me to consider publishing a book on the topic of overcoming The Affair, lust. May the pages in this book 'help break every cycle of guilt and shame throughout this world! Through Christ, may no one ever be alone.' Thank you!

Joseph's Ministry.

I am grateful for your 'Yes'. Thank you for helping me to share my journey with The Affair to the world to be a resource of managing sex in singleness…God's way. May God bless every person who is a part of your team.

I believe this is just the beginning to Breaking Cycles.

Testimonials

This section is dedicated to an anonymous community who are choosing either the celibacy and abstinence lifestyle. Each person I asked what helpful tips would they like to share to help in choosing purity and why did they choose a season of purity.

May their journey encourage you in your own!

Anonymous- Hockley, TX
Exercising is one of the things that helps me to sustain purity in my life.

Anonymous-New York, NY
Worshiping throughout the day through music. The peace and clarity makes a clear pathway for you and God to connect #nostatic

Why purity: I want to get back to what God intended for my life. It's never too late to turn your life around for the better. Also, I want to pour from a better cup.

Anonymous-
Reading my Bible and praying helped me make the decision, and continues to help me sustain purity. I made the decision because I was tired of the relationship cycles.

When I was living in lust, I realized that the feelings were never lasting because they were built on the wrong things. As God revealed to me how He sees me, I no longer desired to devalue myself to fulfill my own sinful desires. I wanted to save that part of myself for someone who saw me as worthy of marriage because of who I am in Christ, instead of giving into lust for temporary pleasure and relationships.

Anonymous-Smyrna, GA
Prayer and NOT dating. I've never been a sexually driven person anyway however I have no temptations because I'm not looking for anything and I don't put myself in situations where I may feel urges. I'm pretty much focused on myself, God, and my personal growth. Even when I start dating again it won't be hard on my end to continue my lifestyle.

I encourage it (purity) because once you have sex, all the common sense floats out of your body LOL. No but seriously, waiting serves value. I believe that's why the Bible says to wait for marriage.

When you can value your body enough to not share it with just anyone there will be meaning behind your intimacy with your husband not only for you but him as well.

Also, you have more clarity when you don't have sex and for me more self-confidence. I lost my virginity at 21 (sorry if that's TMI) and mentally justified my choice to be intimate because he would be "my husband" one day.

Well, that ship sunk so now I'm back abstaining from sex because that's what my intentions and beliefs were in the first place. I'm more mature now, I know better and I know what I expect out of myself and I know what God expects out of me.

Anonymous
Prayer, fasting, not being alone with men or trying to stay busy (the devil finds work for idlers)

The peace is like no other. Not worrying about certain things and just being one with yourself and the creator you get so much stronger! I chose it because I was unhappy fornicating 5 mins of sex and days of depression and worrying

Anonymous from Tulsa, OK
SLEEP lol that helps, no but honestly one thing, stay out of my bed unless it is time to sleep. It took a while to notice how that has kept me from a wandering mind, and always playing music that didn't entice me.

Being fruitfully honest, I'd only encourage someone who's made it a consideration or is wrestling with the sex life that they have. Everyone isn't Christian and I don't want to force that on them, but if the invitation is open for how Abstinence is beneficial in that time of their life? Then I'm all for it!

I have been abstinent for a decade nearly, and it was easy for me. God preserved me and kept me from a number of close calls back then, but I never had the "pressures" to have sex.

The longer I was in it, the easier I saw my life. Less traps / able to see things from a more objective POV / no children or attachments to anyone I didn't need to remain stuck with / no ties and so on...compared to others who were always having sex. I'd much rather wait. Just was me to live this way.

Sources

1. vocabulary.com: "If you are earnest, it means you are serious about something."
2. Bible Gateway: Ecclesiastes 4:9
3. Youversion Bible Plan (But Seek Ye First The Kingdom of God)
4. The Bible Detox Dr. Dharius Daniels
5. Facts on gold: https://www.epmf.be/precious-metal-all-around-you/
https://www.gold.org/about-gold/gold-supply/how-gold-is-mined

About The Author

Breonna 'BG' Gildon is a fervent fan of God, family, and faith. Her words bring life through the purpose of sharing transparency to empower throughout the world. She leads Empower Her Blog and its faithful tribe, Honey Bunches, where its vision is "Sharing Transparency To Empower!"

Breonna has written faith based ebooks and collaborated recently in an anthropology for young women called, The Cards of Life: Finding Your Winning Hand.

The Affair is Breonna's first solo published book. You can learn more about Breonna and her ministry Empower Her by visiting bgempowers.com or enjoy her gospel-related content on TikTok by following her @bgempowers !

www.ingramcontent.com/pod-product-compliance
Lightning Source LLC
Chambersburg PA
CBHW051449290426
44109CB00016B/1682